Close Your Eyes So You Can See

Stories of Children in the Life of Jesus

MICHAEL CARD

ILLUSTRATIONS BY
STEPHEN MARCHESI

Harvest House Publishers
Eugene, Oregon 97402

Card, Michael, 1957-
    Close your eyes so you can see / by Michael Card: illustrated by Stephen Marchesi.
    p. cm.
    Summary: The daughter of Jarius, the boy with the five loaves and two fishes, and other young people in the New Testament relate events involving children in the life of Jesus.
    ISBN 1-56507-425-4 (hardcover: alk. paper)
    1. Children's stories, American. 2. Jesus Christ—Juvenile fiction. [1. Jesus Christ—Fiction.
2. Christian life—Fiction. 3. Short stories.] I. Marchesi, Stephen, ill. II. Title. P27.C1895C1 1996
    [Fic]—dc20
                                                                96-11616
                                                                CIP
                                                                AC

Design and production by Left Coast Design, Portland, Oregon

Scripture verses are from the Holy Bible, New International Version R. Copyright © 1973, 1978, 1984 by the International Bible Society. Used by permission of Zondervan Publishing House. The "NIV" and "New International Version" trademarks are registered in the United States Patent and Trademark Office by International Bible Society.

Printed in Mexico.

96 97 98 99 00 01 02 03 04 05 / 10 9 8 7 6 5 4 3 2

Dear Mom and Dad,

The eyes of little children see so much more than grownup eyes see. Perhaps this is one reason why Jesus, who cared so much about seeing, was drawn to children. Children are able to understand, it seems, without thinking, without the strained rationalizing that we adults need to go through. Little ones can "see" more with their eyes closed than we can with telescopes and binoculars.

As you travel through the pages of the gospels, you'll notice that children are important to Jesus. He speaks to them, takes time for them, even lives His life as one of them. He uses children as examples in His teaching, and they seem to always be somewhere close by, playing, shouting, perhaps even listening.

Jesus taught us, His grownup followers, that what we need to be is children! That we need to learn to accept the free gifts of grace He offers. That we need to stop arguing about who is the greatest. We need to believe like children, with simple, uncluttered trust, because a fully mature disciple is the one with the heart of a child.

These stories are fictional adaptations of the actual children who appear in the narratives of the New Testament. They seek to provide a point of contact for today's children to those first-century children who actually saw and knew Jesus. I hope that young readers, by way of their imaginations, will hear for themselves Jesus' words to children, that they will see, on their own, what a treasure they are to Him and what a tremendous gift it is to be a child who knows and follows Him.

It is my prayer that we all might see with our eyes closed.

...that we should be called children of God. For we are!

1 John 3:1

Close Your Eyes
So You Can See

There's a way that a child
Can look at the world
And see through the eyes of the heart.
They see meaning beyond the mystery,
Hear the silence of the stars.

So close your eyes so you can see
The way He meant this world to be,
And understand with childlike heart,
The place we end is where we start.

The child is the father of the man;
It's the paradox of God's design.
So if you would be grown up and mature,
Let the light of your childhood shine.

So close your eyes so you can see
what it must be like to be
A little girl or boy who knows
And walks with Jesus as they grow.

When Jesus Was a Boy 7

LUKE 2:41-52

Who Is the Greatest? 11

MATTHEW 18:1-5

Little Girl, Arise 15

MARK 5:21-42

Learning to Share 19

JOHN 6:5-13

Let the Children Come! 25

MARK 10:13-16

Taking Jesus at His Word 29

JOHN 4:46-53

The Bully's Tune 33

LUKE 7:31-35

Hosanna 37

MATTHEW 21:12-16

The Girl at the Gate 41

JOHN 18:15-18, 25-27

Opening the Door 45

ACTS 12:1-17

When Jesus Was a Boy

LUKE 2:41-52

C*lose your eyes so you can see a great marble building perched on top of a hill. It is called the Temple, and it is here that everyone comes to worship God. Listen to the voices of a large crowd standing all around the huge building. Feel the scratchy fabric of the clothes against your arm as people brush by you, on their way up the hill.*

It is Passover, a special time of celebration. Everyone is coming to Jerusalem to give their offerings and prayers at the Temple. Two of the people in the crowd are Joseph and Mary. Watch them as they ask every person, "Have you seen our boy? Have you seen Jesus?"

A small crowd of men had gathered by one of the huge pillars that held up the enormous roof of the great Temple. They were very wise men, teachers of the Law in the Temple. In the middle of the group stood a small, barefoot boy. He was asking questions and listening carefully to the answers the wise teachers gave Him. Then He would ask still more questions. It was as if the teachers, in listening to their own answers, were being taught. They were learning from the questions of the boy.

The boy was Jesus.

He had spent two nights in the Temple, sleeping on the floor. During that time, His parents had been frantically searching for Him, carefully retracing their steps from the moment they first realized He was missing. But Jesus wasn't worried. He wasn't even afraid. He trusted that God His Father would take care of Him.

And on this day, in the middle of His discussion with the wise teachers, the young Jesus heard the echoing sound of two sets of hurried footsteps coming closer and closer. He looked past the teachers. Joseph and Mary were rushing toward Him.

The look of relief on their faces when they finally saw the little One they had been searching for was beyond words. In an instant, all their worry, anger, and fear vanished. They had found Jesus! He was sitting on the floor in the midst of the teachers with an innocent but understanding smile on His face.

"We have been looking everywhere for you!" Mary said, out of breath.

"Why were you looking everywhere? Didn't you know that I would be here, in My Father's house?" Jesus asked innocently.

Joseph didn't say a word, though there were tears in his eyes. He simply took Jesus into his arms and carried him all the way back home to Nazareth.

Jesus never strayed from His parents again, for He was a perfectly obedient child.

And Mary and Joseph never misplaced Jesus again, for they were wonderful parents.

And those wise teachers never forgot the lessons they learned from the questions of the curious boy with the questioning eyes.

Asking Questions

Can you imagine what kind of questions Jesus was asking the teachers?

When you have questions, who do you ask?

What kinds of things can you learn by asking questions?

CHAPTER 9

Who Is the Greatest?

MATTHEW 18:1-5

Close your eyes so you can see two small houses by the sea. Can you hear the sound of the waves outside the door? Can you smell the saltiness of the sea?

The sky is dark, the streets are dark, and the houses are almost all dark too. But in one of the homes, you can see a few dim lights shining through the curtainless window. Listen and you can hear the muffled sounds of voices.

His parents named him Rufus because of his red hair ("rufus" means red). He was a quiet boy, the youngest in his large family. Their house in Capernaum was right next door to the little house where Jesus lived—when He was not on the road preaching and teaching and healing.

When Jesus was at home, there was usually a crowd of people at the front door. Sometimes Rufus would go to Jesus' house to see all the different faces. Most especially he liked seeing Jesus' face and hearing the stories He would tell.

One evening, just after supper, Rufus heard voices next door. Then he heard Jesus' warm, familiar voice. Asking permission from his father, Rufus went over to see what was happening.

Jesus recognized Rufus as he stuck his head in the door. He greeted the small boy with a gentle smile and kind words, offering him a piece of bread.

"No, thank You," Rufus said. "I just ate."

"Very well then," Jesus placed the bread back in the basket, "you are welcome to stay."

The way Jesus spoke to Rufus made him feel like the most important person in the world! The small boy moved out of the way and into his usual corner. As he sat down, he heard some of the men around him whispering angrily.

"I gave up my nets and boats," one big man was saying.

"Well, so did I," another interrupted. "And I left a family too!"

"Time will tell," the first said in a solemn voice. "I'm sure that *I* will be known as the greatest follower of Jesus."

Rufus wondered why they were arguing. It seemed a silly thing to do with Jesus in the room.

Just then, Jesus turned and spoke to the men. "What are you bickering about? You're not arguing about who is the greatest again, are you?"

The men looked surprised. They stood in embarrassed silence, waiting to hear what Jesus might say next. No one would answer His question.

Things were beginning to feel a bit tense, so Rufus thought it best to head home. As he was tiptoeing quietly to the door, Jesus called him by name.

"Rufus, will you come here by Me?" Jesus reached out to Rufus and tenderly touched his shoulder. His hands reminded Rufus of his father's hands. They were strong and gentle at the same time.

"Why must you argue about who is the greatest?" Jesus was looking down at Rufus, stroking his hair, but He was speaking to His followers. They didn't say a word.

"Unless you change and become like this little child, don't even bother thinking about entering the Kingdom of Heaven," Jesus said firmly. Every time He emphasized a word, He would move His hand, jiggling Rufus' little red head.

"What?" Rufus looked up, surprised. "You say they are supposed to be like me?" he asked, taking a big breath as he spoke.

Jesus was quiet for a moment, pausing thoughtfully before He spoke. "Tell me, red-haired one," He finally said, "do you love your father?"

"Why, yes," Rufus answered without hesitation.

"Do you try to please him?" Jesus asked.

"Him and no one else," the boy beamed.

"One more question." Jesus bent down on one knee and tenderly placed Rufus' face in His hands. "Do you care about being the greatest?" He quietly asked.

Rufus thought for a moment, wanting to pause the way Jesus did. He could tell this was a very important question. "No, I don't care about being great," Rufus looked into Jesus' eyes, "because my father is great."

Jesus enfolded Rufus in His arms. He looked up at His followers, the warmth of His glance meeting their confused faces. "If you really want to be great, important, grown-up men, then be like this little child whose only concern is pleasing his father."

The men were silent. As Jesus straightened Himself, he snatched Rufus up into His arms. Looking him level in the face, He said with a smile, "I have a great Father too."

Asking Questions

In this story, Jesus lived next door to Rufus. Where does He live now?

Would you have liked to sit in and listen to Jesus speak?

How would Jesus answer the question, "Who is the greatest?"

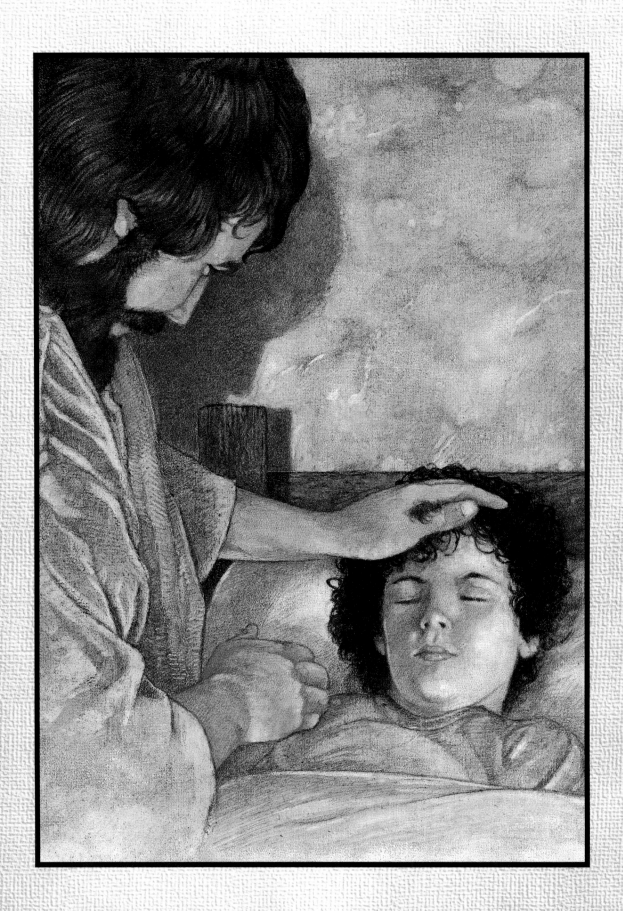

Little Girl, Arise

MARK 5:21-24, 35-43

Close your eyes so you can see a little girl lying very, very still on a small mat in a dark room. Listen to the sounds of a mother and father crying for their only daughter. See the worried father as he leaves the house in search of One who might, even now, make his daughter well. Listen carefully and you might be able to hear his footsteps get softer and softer in the distance as he runs to find Jesus.

The last sound I remember was the sobbing of my father, Jairus. It made me afraid to see him crying. I was so sick and confused. Father had been by my bed the whole time I was sick, leaving only long enough to eat. His worried, fearful face was the last thing I saw as I drifted away. After that there was only a friendly...cool...dark...silence.

When it looked as if there were no hope for me, my father went to look for Jesus. He had heard from one of our servants how Jesus had been healing the sick, how He had helped others who seemed to have no chance of ever getting well. Some of the people who had gathered at the house rolled their eyes when they heard my father had gone to find Jesus. "That crazy preacher from Nazareth?" they shook their heads. "Well, after all, Jairus is desperate."

Finally my father found Jesus. He fell down before Him, begging Him to come home and lay His hands on me to heal me. Jesus didn't say a word. He smiled, turned away from the group of people He was talking to, and walked off with my father. My father was so happy that Jesus would come right away, but as they walked along together, the fear began to rise in his heart again. He thought of the worst that might still happen. What if Jesus couldn't heal me? What if it was already too late?

As they were making their way back to our house, some of our servants met them on the road. The looks on their faces told both Jesus and my father that the worst had happened. They were too late. I had already fallen asleep in death.

"Sir," one of the servants said to my father, "perhaps it's best not to bother Jesus anymore."

When Jesus heard this, He grabbed my father's arm and pulled him close. "Don't be afraid," He whispered in my father's ear, "just believe."

My father was speechless! He didn't know whether to cry or laugh. "Just believe?" he muttered in confusion. "Just believe what?"

My father's steps were heavy as he led Jesus the rest of the way home. When they finally arrived, Jesus asked three of His followers to come inside with Him, along with my parents.

As Jesus was going through the door, He looked over at the people who had come to the house. Many of them had begun to weep.

"Why are you crying?" Jesus asked them with a puzzled expression. "The little girl is not dead, only asleep."

They didn't know how to respond. Some thought it was a cruel joke. Others wondered if Jesus hadn't heard that I had died. Some of them laughed at Him.

When I awoke from the sleep of death, it was Jesus' face I first saw. His words, "Little girl, get up!" were the first words I heard. He was leaning over my little mat on the floor. I could feel the warmth of His hands on my cold forehead. Of all the bewildered and confused-looking faces around my bed, His face alone was calm and sure, simple and smiling. Knowing I was hungry, Jesus told the servants to get something for me to eat. He laughed to see them scurry off to the kitchen in a panic.

Later my father told me how afraid he had been. That he feared he had lost me forever and would never see me again. I never thought that fathers could be so scared.

He told me the story, again and again, about leading Jesus to our house and how Jesus had touched his shoulder and said, "Don't be afraid. Just believe."

My father must have been listening, because from that day he believed in Jesus of Nazareth, and he was never afraid again.

Asking Questions

What are you afraid of?

Was Jairus afraid of death before he met Jesus? What about after he met Jesus?

What does Jesus say to do when we're afraid?

Learning to Share

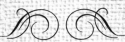

JOHN 6:5-13

Close your eyes so you can see a small house by the sea. Can you hear the soft breathing of a little boy asleep in his simple bed? Can you smell breakfast cooking in the next room? Do you feel the warmth of the morning sun on your face as it creeps in the window?

Outside listen to the sounds of the city of Bethsaida coming to life: merchants calling out, stubborn donkeys braying beneath their burdens, women chatting as they carry water, hungry sea gulls calling as they follow the fishing boats into shore.

As Nathan awoke, the morning surrounded him like a song, and his first thought was of the sea. He scurried through the kitchen, bumping into his mother on the way out the door.

"Nathan! Your breakfast!" his mother called after him.

"I'll eat later!" Nathan replied over his shoulder. "I have to go!"

As he ran into town, Nathan could see the blue of the lake and smell its salty scent. He could hear the voices of the fishermen drifting across the water as they made their way in from their long night's labor. Among the group would be the one person Nathan most wanted to see and hear—his father.

The little boy turned a corner and saw a mass of people standing along the shore. This early in the morning there were usually only tired fishermen and a few noisy gulls. But this crowd seemed to say that someone special was coming to Bethsaida, that they were there to meet Him.

But Nathan's special someone was nowhere to be seen.

And so he decided to wait there for his father. Nathan leaned against one of the cool, whitewashed buildings that looked like it was waiting beside the lake, like Nathan, for someone special to come.

As he waited, daydreaming, Nathan looked down and, to his amazement, a silver coin lay at his feet. When he bent over to retrieve it, a smiling woman saw him and said, "What, a miracle? Have you heard that some people are even finding coins in the mouths of fishes these days!" She laughed. "Boy, you can't eat a miracle, you know."

With coin in hand, Nathan decided to walk over to a booth in the market-place where bread was sold.

"That will buy five of these barley loaves," said the old baker woman, a distant aunt of the little boy.

"Thank you," Nathan replied as he tucked the hard, crusty rolls into a fold of his coat. "I'll share these with my father."

He walked back to his waiting spot on the shore, and to his joy he saw the faded green boat that belonged to his father. But there was no sign of his dad. Another fisherman who worked on the same boat was standing by, washing his nets.

"Have you seen my father?" Nathan called out in his small voice.

"I believe he followed the crowd, in that direction," was the old man's reply. "Here, you look hungry." With that, he tossed two small fish to Nathan, which he expertly caught.

"Thank you!" he shouted over his shoulder as he ran off in the direction the old fisherman pointed.

As Nathan neared a large, grassy field just outside of town, he heard a sound almost like the sound of the waves in the sea (only he knew the sea was in the other direction). He topped a small hill and saw a huge gathering of people. Everyone in town must have been there!

Just then, a young man came running up to him in a panic. "Do you have any food with you?" he asked, out of breath.

"I have a couple of fish and some bread, but I was saving them for my father." Nathan held his elbow tight over the food that was tucked away in the folds of his coat.

"Could you share it with me?" the man asked in a pitiful voice.

Nathan took out one of the fish and a single piece of bread to share, but when the man saw how little the fish was and how small the barley bread, he frowned. "This is hopeless!"

"Wait," Nathan said. "You might as well take it all." With that he handed over the five loaves and two fish.

"Thank you, little one," the man said as he disappeared into the crowd.

Nathan continued to look for his father, walking through all the men, women, boys, and girls who had gathered at the grassy field. As he looked from face to face, Nathan noticed a man sitting in the middle of the crowd. He looked so simple and very friendly. He was telling stories about fishing, which the fishermen loved hearing, and about farming, which the farmers loved hearing, and about making bread, to which all of the women nodded their heads in understanding.

At the same time, Nathan saw his father standing directly behind the storyteller. The worried man he had given his food to had interrupted a story about a farmer sowing seed. He was handing over the fish and bread.

"This is all I could find," he said with a very sad expression.

"Call the Twelve," the storyteller replied, "and pass out the food to everyone."

He motioned to some other men who were standing by. They all had baskets in their hands. They gathered in a tight circle around the storyteller. There was a moment of silence, and Nathan understood that the man in the center of the crowd was giving thanks to God for the food.

When the prayer was over, each man moved off in a different direction, filling the lunch baskets of everyone in the crowd. The men who were passing out the food had surprised looks on their faces. They kept looking back toward the man who had called them together and blessed the food. The fish and loaves never ran out! Nathan was amazed. It was a miracle.

The crowd, though, didn't know anything had happened. They clamored only for the food.

At last Nathan made his way alongside his father, who was munching on one of the crusty rolls.

"I've been looking for you," his father said to him with a kind smile. "Here, have something to eat." Even his father did not understand that the food he had just received from the disciples was special—it was part of a miracle.

As Nathan took some bread, he noticed a shadow come across his father's face. He was looking at someone who was standing behind Nathan.

"Jesus," his father whispered.

Nathan turned to see the storyteller, the one who had blessed the few fish and loaves and made them many.

"You are Nathan," Jesus said, looking down at the small boy.

"I saw what You did with the fish and bread, sir," Nathan whispered, out of breath. "You did a miracle!"

Jesus smiled, shielding His eyes from the hot, noonday sun. He bent down on one knee, putting his arms around the boy. Nathan could smell the fish on His hands and the dust in His hair. Jesus pulled him close and whispered in his ear, "And you, my little son, helped!"

Asking Questions

What happened when Nathan shared his loaves and fish?

Have you ever had something extra-special happen because you were willing to share?

Nathan's father didn't know the bread he ate was part of a miracle, but Nathan did. Do you think it's easy or hard to recognize miracles?

CHAPTER
5

Let the Children Come!

MARK 10:13-16

C lose your eyes so you can see the warm sun shining on a group of parents waiting with their young children, waiting to see Jesus. Hear some of them grumbling at having to wait so long. See some of the mothers shifting their babies from one arm to the other. Can you smell which one of the babies has a dirty diaper? Watch the disciples trying to shoo the people away.

O ur parents wanted us to meet Jesus, to have Him pray for us. It is our custom to ask a visiting teacher to pray for the children. We call it the "barocha," a blessing.

I had heard many things about Jesus, that He had made sick people well and blind people see, that He said things and did things like no one else. I was curious to meet such a person. What would He look like? How would He act? Would He notice me?

Suddenly, the disciples who were with Jesus came over to our group and said, "Go away! Jesus is tired and busy. He has no time for children."

After all this waiting, I wasn't going to even see Him! I began to sniffle back some tears. When Jesus heard me, He turned from the people He was speaking to and walked toward us.

"I will see the children," He told the disciples in a firm voice. "Don't you know that God's kingdom is for children just like this?" His face lit up as He spoke those last few words.

He joined our group and got down on His knees so He could look us straight in the face. He told us stories and little jokes we could understand. He laughed and played with us while the disciples looked on, some of them looking a little embarrassed to see Jesus rolling on the ground and playing games with us.

But my sadness went away. I had met Jesus.

Finally, our parents began to get impatient. They reminded Jesus of why we had come: to have Him say a prayer for our group.

When our parents stopped the game-playing, I saw Jesus give them a disappointed look. I think maybe He wanted to play more.

We began forming a circle around Jesus so He might pray for all of us at once. But Jesus took us, one at a time, placing His hands on our head and praying for us individually. His prayers were different for each one of us. He knew our names, though no one had told him. He called some of us by new names.

I was last in line, and by the time Jesus came to me, I didn't know what to say or do.

"You are called Michael," He said to me, smiling. "But I will call you Isaac, because your life will be full of laughter."

He placed His hands on my head and looked up to heaven. "Father," He said, "be with Michael this day. I ask that You care for and protect him, according to Your will. Make him strong so he can serve You better. Amen."

He took me off His lap and was just about to push me in the direction of my mother when He stopped and placed His hands on my head. "Oh, and Father, give him joy."

As I grew older, I often wondered what Jesus' blessing meant. Then one day I learned who Jesus was—that He was the Messiah and He had died for me. That day I became one of His followers. I remembered what He had said about the Kingdom of God belonging to children, and all at once I realized that I was His child too. The Kingdom of God was mine! And then I began to laugh. From that day on my life was filled with joy, just as Jesus had asked.

And from that day on I asked everyone to call me Isaac.

Asking Questions

If Jesus prayed for you right now, what do you think He would ask God for?

What kind of game would you like to have played with Jesus?

If Jesus were to give you a new name, what would you like it to be?

Taking Jesus at His Word

JOHN 4:46-53

C lose your eyes so you can see a large white house made of
stone. It towers above all the other houses in town. Listen as a
worried father leaves by the front door and runs down the
street. See the dust rise up in small clouds behind him as his feet pound
the dirt road. Watch as two servants burst out the door, looking for him
both ways down the street. As they turn to follow, the man's wife appears
at the door. Hear the sounds of her crying.

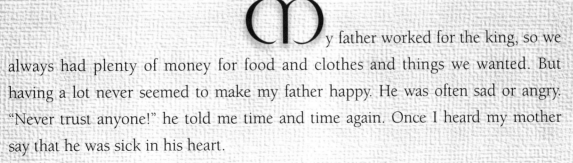

y father worked for the king, so we
always had plenty of money for food and clothes and things we wanted. But
having a lot never seemed to make my father happy. He was often sad or angry.
"Never trust anyone!" he told me time and time again. Once I heard my mother
say that he was sick in his heart.

Since I was the only child of my father and mother, I was given almost anything

I desired. I even had a servant who waited on me hand and foot. But none of these things really made me happy either.

One day I started feeling sick. My head hurt and I felt so hot. By the next day I was in bed. By the end of the week, my parents called the doctor. But he just shook his head and said there wasn't anything he could do for me.

One of the servants told my father that he had heard of a man, Jesus of Nazareth, who could heal the sick. The servant also told us that many people were saying this Jesus had raised someone from the dead.

"Where can I find this man?" my father asked desperately.

"He's in Cana," replied one of the servants.

That instant my father ran out the door. He did not take the time to prepare for the long trip. He did not pack several bags with food and clothes for the journey as he usually did. He didn't even command the servants to come along—though two of them did follow him out the door and down the road.

They arrived at Cana, out of breath from running most of the way, just as it was getting dark. Going from house to house, they frantically asked if anyone knew where this Jesus could be found. Finally, an old woman directed them to the house where Jesus was staying.

When they arrived at the house, there were no lights on inside. It looked as though everyone had gone to sleep. My father started banging on the door.

"Jesus! Jesus! My son is sick! He's going to die!" he shouted in the darkness through the closed door. My father had been worrying about me all the way to Cana, afraid that even now he might be too late.

Jesus came to the door scratching His head and wiping the sleep from His eyes.

"Come, before my son dies!" my father blurted out, almost in tears. "I will pay any price you ask. Just make my son well."

Jesus spoke slowly, as if he thought my father couldn't hear very well. "You can go," He said, looking my father straight in the eye. "Your son will live." His voice calmed my father's fear. And He didn't mention wanting any money.

Exhausted and dazed, my father turned as if he were in a dream. He dropped his money bag in the dust and walked away into the night. Something about Jesus had convinced him that I would be all right. Something in his heart heard and understood. He took Jesus at His word.

I was waiting for my father at the front door the next morning as he and the two servants came stumbling into the house. They were so tired after traveling all night. And although my father was grateful to see me healed, he did not act at all surprised that I was better. He had met the servants who had been sent with the good news that I was well. I had been instantly healed at the exact moment Jesus told my father I would live.

"I took Jesus at His word," my father later said to me. "His voice, the look on His face, everything about Him told me I could trust His word was true. And so I trusted. I took Him at His word, and His word healed your body and my soul." He took me in his arms and held me close.

I knew then that Jesus had not only made me well, but He had made my father truly happy for the very first time in his life. And that was more special to me than all the money in the world.

Asking Questions

Did money make the father happy?

What did it mean for the father to take Jesus at His word? What does it mean for us?

How had the father changed at the end of the story?

The Bully's Tune

LUKE 7:31-35

Close your eyes so you can see a busy marketplace. Listen to the voices of a hundred people speaking all at once, shouting out the things they have to sell, arguing about the prices they have to pay. Smell the dust that hangs in the air as people shuffle from place to place. Does your mouth water at the sight of the bread and fruits for sale? Hear a group of children playing on the street corner. Watch as Jesus and His disciples approach the children.*

35

It was market day in Capernaum, so everyone in the city was there. My friends and I had been playing chase all morning, and we were very tired. Running in-between all the busy people in the market, bumping into baskets of fish and bread, trying to make it back to home base before you got caught—all these things can wear a person out!

That's when Nahu, the biggest of our group (and sometimes a bully), said, "Everyone, look what I have." He pulled a small flute from his pocket.

"Where did you get that?" I asked in amazement.

"I found it," was all he would say.

"Probably stole it," Micah whispered under his breath. Nahu ignored him.

Though he didn't know the first thing about playing it, Nahu put the flute to his big lips and began to blow, his cheeks puffing all the way out. With one hand he began to make great circles in the air, trying to get us to dance.

"Now get in a circle," he ordered. "And dance until the music stops."

"That's not music," I complained. "It's just noise."

He pulled the flute from his teeth for a split second to bark out, "Dance!" and then he went back to his noise-making.

We all stood, arms folded, heads to one side, refusing to go along with this silly game.

Nahu angrily threw down the flute in the dust, breaking off one end. "I said DANCE!" he yelled in his big brutish voice, his big red face two inches from my own. "I am the biggest, and so what I say you will do!"

"We aren't going to dance to your silly music," I said, summoning up a courage I didn't know I had.

From the way Nahu looked at me, I thought he was going to pick a fight. But then he backed away and looked around at the others. "Then let's pretend we're at a funeral. I'll sing a sad song, and you pretend to be mourners."

"You mean like bury a grasshopper?" I said.

"What's a mourner?" piped up little Levi.

"A sad person at a funeral," I explained to him.

"That doesn't sound like much..."Levi began, but Nahu's glare silenced him.

It was clear Nahu didn't care what we played. He just wanted to make all the rest of us do what he said. Whether we were having any fun didn't matter to him. He wanted our obedience, and he would get it any way he could.

And so he began to sing a song which sounded so bad it actually made me want to mourn for a moment. The other kids glanced at each other with puzzled looks on their faces.

"This isn't any fun," one little girl whined.

"You will play the game because I say so!" Nahu growled.

A few of us tried to play along, more out of fear than anything else. We rubbed our eyes with our fists and pretended to cry. My pet turtle had died a week before, so I tried to think about him—but it didn't work.

"I've had enough," I said at last and walked away.

"Come back or else!" Nahu shouted but he didn't follow me. I think he was afraid of losing the other kids if he left the group. That's when I saw a group of men standing beside the road. They looked like they had been watching us.

"Isn't that what grownups are like?" one man said, smiling at me as I passed by. "Everyone wants you to dance to their tune. If they say dance a jig, they want you to do it. If they say cry out loud, they expect everyone to go along."

"But Jesus," someone in the group said, "what do You mean?"

"Don't listen to them," the man called Jesus told the others around Him. "John the Baptist didn't dance to their tune, and neither will I. Be brave, like this little one who walked away and refused to dance to the bully's tune."

Jesus' voice got louder as I walked away. I could tell He meant for me to hear His words as well as the men around Him. In the background I could still hear Nahu making horrible noises, but I decided from then on I would only listen to Jesus' voice.

Asking Questions

Would you have done what Nahu wanted the kids to do?

How was the little boy being brave when he walked away?

Do you know how to listen to Jesus' voice? How does He talk to us today?

hosanna

Close your eyes so you can see a group of Gentile children *running through the marbled halls of one of the courtyards of the Temple, the huge stone building where everyone came to worship God. Listen to their shouts of joy. "Hosanna to the Son of David," they yell at the top of their lungs. It is Passover time, a special celebration of what God had done for His people. See the angry expressions of the priests and teachers of the Law as they glare at the noisy children and then at Jesus.*

We followed the crowd of Jews in from the city gate. At the head of the mass of people was Jesus, sitting on a young donkey. His feet were dragging the ground from time to time, so small was the donkey.

At the Temple He dismounted, walked to the great door, and went inside. He entered the Gentile court, where our parents were trying to pray. Our families were not Jewish, but we believed in God, and this courtyard was our special place. As Jesus walked through, He saw that the priests had set up the Temple market in the middle of the only place in the Temple where we were allowed to pray.

Our parents were trying their best to pray, but everyone was shouting and arguing about the prices of the goods in the market. I saw my father finally give up. He rose from his knees and was about to leave the courtyard.

"Everyone knows the market belongs outside the holy Temple," he complained as he rolled up the small piece of carpet he used to kneel on, "but no one is brave enough to confront the priests who moved it inside."

We had just made our way out of the great door when all of a sudden we heard the loud "baa" of sheep. We turned, and there were dozens of sheep coming out the door! Then doves began flying out as fast as they could. Next came fists full of silver coins and then the merchants themselves, one by one, chasing after their merchandise.

Finally Jesus came and stood at the door, shouting after them. "This is a place of prayer, not a shopping mall!" His face was flushed, but He seemed satisfied. Turning to go back into the Temple, He motioned for my family to follow. My parents were smiling on account of what Jesus had done for them. At last they had a quiet place to talk to God.

Groups of my relatives were gathered around Jesus, thanking Him for clearing our court of the noisy merchants. When my friends and I saw our families thanking Jesus, we started to run back and forth, singing and shouting, "Hosanna!" That word means "Oh save!" and we always shouted it at Passover. The noise we were making was the right kind of noise, "a joyful noise," Jesus said with a laugh.

Jesus was sitting on the low stone wall that separated our special place in the Temple from the other courts. He was watching us run back and forth. Sometimes He would even clap His hands and join in our songs.

Just then, a group of priests, dressed in black from head to toe, came up to Jesus with angry expressions on their faces.

"Tell them to be quiet!" one of the priests barked at Jesus. "Do you hear what they are saying?"

We stopped shouting, afraid that we had gotten Jesus into trouble.

"What they are saying is perfect," Jesus said, still looking at us and smiling.

Asking Questions

Why did the servant girl let Peter in?

Why was John angry and hurt when Peter said what he said?

What do you think went through Peter's mind when he looked across
the courtyard and saw Jesus?

10

Opening the Door

ACTS 12:1-17

Close your eyes so you can see a circle of people praying on their knees. In one corner of the dark room there is a simple oil lamp, casting a warm, yellow glow. Hear the whispers of their prayers as they ask the Lord for a miracle. See how they occasionally look up while no one else is watching to see if there is truly hope on each other's faces.

Outside the circle there is a little girl. She is twelve, and her name is Rhoda. She is not looking up but has her eyes clamped shut. Like the others, she is asking God for the impossible.

We had just heard of Herod's decision to take Peter to trial after the Passover. We all knew what this would mean. A trial for a follower of Jesus was no trial at all—merely a meeting to pass a sentence of death.

45

All the believers had come to the house of my mistress, Mary (John Mark's mother), to pray for Peter. We were asking for a miracle, for the Lord to send His angels to rescue Peter from prison.

It was getting late when John Mark said, "We should rest now and trust God to care for His servant, our brother Peter."

Just as we were rising from our knees, we heard a soft knocking at the door. We looked at each other. Everyone had been careful to make sure they had not been followed by soldiers or spies, but still we feared it might be someone come to arrest us, too, for being believers in Jesus of Nazareth.

"Answer it," Mary whispered to me fearfully. I tiptoed to the outer door and stood for a moment, straining to see if I could hear a clatter of swords or armor. But all I could hear was the heavy breathing of a single man, alone in the dark. I pressed my hands against the thick wooden door and whispered, "Who is there?"

"It is I," the deep male voice whispered back. It was Peter's voice!

"Oh, my!" I shouted and ran back into the main room, leaving Peter outside in the dark.

"It's Peter!" I said, jumping up and down with excitement. "He's at the door!"

Everyone gasped in amazement.

"What?"

"Child, you're out of your mind."

"Impossible!"

"It couldn't be!"

"Shhhhh!"

"But isn't that what we were just praying for?" I asked. "I am only a child and don't know the faith as well as you grownups, but why shouldn't God hear and answer our prayers this very night?"

"Maybe it's Peter's guardian angel," someone said. "Would he have a voice like Peter's?"

John Mark spoke up. "So, you can believe there is an angel standing at the door but not Peter?" There was a frown on his face. "Five minutes ago we were all praying and asking the Lord to rescue Peter from prison. How is it that now you have so little faith? I believe with Rhoda that God has heard our prayers."

Just then we heard another knock at the door. This time it was not so soft.

"Oh," I said. "I forgot Peter!"

I ran back and threw open the door. There he stood, almost shining in the darkness. It was Peter. He took my hand in his, and together we walked into the room.

Everyone started speaking at once.

"How did...?"

"Where were you...?"

"What happened?"

Peter placed one of his big fingers to his lips. "Shhh," he said. "They will be looking for me by now."

He explained how, at the very time we were praying for his release, an angel appeared and poked him in the side to wake him up. Peter thought he was dreaming. The angel touched the chains on his hand and feet, and they simply fell to the ground with a clank. But the guards who were chained to him on either side didn't move. The angel led Peter through the crowd of sleeping guards and toward the entrance of the prison.

"When we came to the heavy iron gate," Peter spoke wide-eyed, "it opened all by itself!"

One of the men rolled his eyes in disbelief.

"Can you not see me standing here in front of you?" Peter snapped. "You asked God, and He sent His angel to rescue me!"

"We should pray," John Mark stepped in, "and thank God for Peter's rescue from the hands of Herod."

We all knelt again, and everyone had their own time of prayer. But Peter just kept whispering, "Thank You, thank You." There were tears in his eyes.

"I must be on my way," Peter said after a long silence. "I am endangering you all."

He rose and looked around the room, tears still in his eyes. "Thank you for your prayers and for believing the Lord would answer them." He placed a big hand on my shoulder. "Walk out with me, Rhoda."

As he reached for the door latch, Peter looked down at me and said, "Never doubt that God will open the door for you, Rhoda, even as you opened the door for me. The air is full of angels whom God will use to deliver us from every prison."

Those were the last words I heard Peter say, whispered to me with a boyish smile on his face.

Asking Questions

Why were the people in the house afraid of the knock at the door?

Though they had been praying for Peter's rescue, who did they think was at the door? Have you ever prayed for something and not really expected God to answer?

Did you know you have a guardian angel?